Sabine Garvey Campbell began writing poetry as a child and featured a collection of her work in the anthology, *The Four Charms: Faith, Hope, Love and Luck*, in February 2017. She then published the first book of the Suzanne Styles series, *Follow Your Heart,* in May 2017. The second book in the series, *The Diamond Heart*, followed in December 2017. In her writings, Sabine shares heartfelt stories of her own life experiences designed to inspire her readers.

Sabine lives in Virginia with her husband and two children.

To Gavin, Killian, and Teagan.
The destination is more than worth the journey.

Sabine Garvey Campbell

An Unexpected Road to Motherhood

AUSTIN MACAULEY PUBLISHERS™

LONDON · CAMBRIDGE · NEW YORK · SHARJAH

Ordering Information:
Quantity sales: special discounts are available on quantity purchases by corporations, associations, and others. For details, contact the publisher at the address below.

Publisher's Cataloging-in-Publication data
Campbell, Sabine Garvey
An Unexpected Road to Motherhood

ISBN 9781645362234 (Paperback)
ISBN 9781645362241 (Hardback)
ISBN 9781645368533 (ePub e-book)

Library of Congress Control Number: 2019918316

www.austinmacauley.com/us

First Published (2020)
Austin Macauley Publishers LLC
40 Wall Street, 28th Floor
New York, NY 10005
USA

mail-usa@austinmacauley.com
+1 (646) 5125767

Chapter 1

I remember the day, my husband proposed to me, like it was yesterday. The memory of that day will never leave me like the last time I saw my father or the day our children were born.

It was a Saturday morning, like any other, when he woke me up early to say he needed to run out. We shared a little house about twenty minutes from town so it was nothing unusual for him to run errands on the weekends. He was acting a little strange that morning but I did not think anything of it.

Given that he knew just about everyone in our small town, I assumed he would be gone for a while. It was quite normal for him to stop for a bite to eat so he could to talk with some of the locals.

I spent the morning in my bathrobe and pajamas cleaning the house. My hair was pulled back in a ratty-looking ponytail and I had old mascara from the night before caked to my eyelashes. Fortunately, I brushed my teeth right after I got out of bed.

It was just before lunchtime when I saw his SUV pull up the long and winding driveway so I tightened my belt and stepped outside to greet him. When he parked, I could see through the front windshield that he had a rather strange look on his face. I descended the staircase to the driveway to investigate.

When I reached the bottom step, the driver's side door slowly opened just before he slipped out of his seat. When his feet hit the ground, he took one-step around the door that was partly ajar looking as if he was about to be sick. His face was flushed and his hands were shaking.

I asked him if he was okay to which he nodded his head yes. Then, I asked him where he had been. He explained that he ran into some friends while he was at the grocery store so they went for a Bloody Mary. I did not care for his explanation so I stood in silence with my arms crossed to convey my displeasure. He then stuck his hand into his pocket and pulled something out. It was a paper ring which he held in the air as he asked me if I wanted to get married.

His tone was slightly arrogant and very self-confident despite the nervousness that I would later learn was churning inside him but I did not mind. That was just his style.

As you might have guessed, I cried and then said yes just before nearly knocking him over with a hug and a kiss.

I had waited years for that day to come and it caught me completely off-guard. He caught me completely off-guard. There was no weekend getaway, no fireworks, and he never did get down on one knee. It was completely by the seat of his pants and utterly unconventional like just about everything he had done since the day we met. That, too, was just his style.

My boyfriend and I had met three years earlier at work. At the time, I was dating someone and he was engaged.

Given the circumstances, neither of us thought much about the other so it was really no surprise we did not talk unless it related to work. Even then, we barely spoke.

A few months later, a co-worker decided to secretly play cupid when she learned we were both unexpectedly single. Without our knowing, she intentionally invited us to be part of a bowling team for a corporate charity event. Over a beer and a bowling game, we finally exchanged our first social words. A few days later, he asked me out on our first official date.

It was a cold, snowy day in February just before Valentine's Day. We were talking over instant messenger about a project to which we had both been assigned. Toward the end of the conversation he asked, what I was doing that evening to which I replied, nothing. I normally just went home after work to let my dogs out. I asked him the same question to be courteous. He replied that he was taking a pretty girl to dinner.

How arrogant of him, I thought. *Why would he tell me such a thing? As if I wanted to know about his dating life.* I quickly tried to close the conversation by wishing him a good evening to which he immediately responded with a single question. He wanted to know what time I could leave work. I was stunned. He did not even ask me out; he just assumed we were going out. I was as flattered as I was irritated and intrigued.

It did not take long for me to figure out that his past was like something you read about in a book and he was the larger than life leading man. As such, he put himself first. He played by his own rules and called all the shots. He was like no man I had ever known and then again, in some ways, he was just like my father. The man was a roller coaster and I had taken a front row seat.

There were always compromises to be made with my unconventional man from the start. First, with spontaneity came altered plans. Second, with impulse decisions came impulse consequences and third, with arrogance came expectations. He expected perfection of himself so he expected it of nearly everyone else (especially me) despite my telling him that perfection was an illusion. He accepted and rewarded nothing less.

He could wake in the morning as the sweetest, most charming man and then transform into the unkindest human being I had ever met. Yet, through it all, he spoke of me to just about anyone who would listen as if I was the best thing that had ever happened to him.

It was not until we moved in together three months later that I came to finally see that his bad-boy persona was not just an act, it was the very nature of his beast. He was very outgoing and personable which meant he was also highly social. At first, I found it to be very intoxicating given that I had enjoyed an active social life before we got together so in that respect, I believed we were perfectly matched. As time passed, I eventually realized that socializing was a large part of his life and had been for years. In fact, it was a very large part. But, by then it was too late. I had already fallen head over heels for the man.

I was so naive that I honestly expected my boyfriend to settle down after we got engaged. By settling down I meant that he would start to curtail his constant need to go out with his friends. When that change did not come by the time we were married, I thought surely that it would happen after he took a wife. Instead, I learned that not all men settle down after they get married and my husband was one of those men.

Like most women, I have always been mature beyond my years so I did what I had hoped of him. I began settling down when we got engaged and then I settled down even more after we married. With three little words, my days of regularly socializing with my single friends were behind me. I was ready for the fairy tale complete with the white picket fence. Unfortunately, the man I married was not but he loved me enough to try to give it to me anyway. The only hitch was that it had to be on his terms and according to his schedule. And, on the day I said, *I do*, I accepted his terms. At the time, I was okay with them but all bets were off on the day our children came into the world.

Chapter 2

When my husband and I first started dating, we worked together but had enough separation to make the relationship work. Once he realized that we could become serious, he left the company for a bigger and better opportunity. He decided to change jobs because I had already reached a manager level and he did not want to interrupt my career path. This moved us to a routine of just seeing each other in the evenings and on weekends like most dating or married couples we knew.

It was not long after, we moved in together that we slowly transitioned to a virtual work environment. At first, we were both just working at home one to two days a week but that eventually led to every day within a few months. We unexpectedly and unintentionally reverted back to a state of being together all the time.

We had both been in enough relationships to know that being with your partner twenty-four hours a day, seven days a week is not healthy for any relationship. But rather than shake things up at work, we decided to make the best of our new situation.

One year later, we moved to a remote mountain community located twenty minutes outside of Boulder,

Colorado. My office was on the second floor either in the family room or in our bedroom while his was on the first floor in a spare bedroom. Since his job required him to be on conference calls nearly the entire day, he needed a door he could shut.

From our office windows, we overlooked mile-upon-mile of the continental divide. We saw far more wild life than we did people and our dogs roamed free since there was never any traffic on our dead-end road of which to speak. It was freeing yet confining. Freeing in that the liberated landscape did nothing to restrict creativity like the four white walls of an office but confining in that it was just the two of us, day in and day out.

For a social person like my boyfriend that lifestyle was a double-edged sword. One the one side, it built the connection with nature that fed his soul but on the other, it made him feel cut-off from society. Something no social butterfly can endure for long periods of time. On some days, it calmed and inspired him then on others it left him feeling anxious and wanting. It was on those days that I recommended he went into the local office but he would not, even though he had the chance.

To calm the troubled waters of his daily routine, he conjured up some excuse nearly every afternoon as to why he had to drive into town. Sometimes, he needed to run to the bank, sometimes he needed to go to the post office or sometimes he just needed to put gas in the car. Whatever his excuse, it was nothing more than a reason to get out of the house.

I, on the other hand, spent days on end in the house because there were always a million things to do and most of them landed on my to-do list. Though I, too, had days when mountain living became a little too desolate even for my tastes and I needed to break out and see people. On those days, I would accompany him to town.

His routine remained the same even after we married roughly one year later. Not even the ring on his left hand, the constant reminder that he had committed himself to the woman he loved, could change that. He even went so far as to come up with an entirely new reason for going out. He tried to convince me that since we were married *and* working at home together, we needed to spend time apart so we could miss one another.

I did not entirely disagree. However, I thought that despite the fact we had been working at home together for years and only saw each other between meetings, meant, we really did not see each other that often. In my opinion, that was what the evenings were all about and that was what married couples did. Married or dating, it made no difference.

So, I started to complain more about being left home alone but it never did any good. In hindsight, I think it actually made the situation worse. It was counterintuitive to me to think that had I just given him the space he said he needed; he would not have so deliberately tried to exert his individuality by going out with his friends. And, he would not have stayed out until all hours of the night.

Since my husband was the second most social person I knew next to my father, he had an absurd number of people in the two closest towns he called, friends. I am sure, he easily had ten friends for every one of mine. Since he knew that many people, his cell phone rang off the hook and his text messages pinged day and night with invitations to this event, that happy hour or some concert at the town music venue. He always knew where and when to be seen and he rarely disappointed.

When I got pregnant a few years later, I became very focused on preparing for our next chapter and I thought he needed to do the same. Especially when, in the beginning of my third trimester, I had minor complications that placed me on bed rest. Since I could rarely leave the house, my husband took it upon himself to run my errands, too. I was thankful to him for doing so but I also knew that my precarious situation gave him just another reason to get out of the house.

Perhaps as his way of trying to smooth things over, along with all the burgers I could eat and milkshakes I could drink, he delivered the news that this friend or that friend asked about me and how I was doing. I honestly believe he thought that knowing people asked about me kept me from feeling lonely but all I heard was that he was meeting up with his friends when he was supposed to be running errands or sitting at home with me.

Over the years, I wondered from time-to-time what my husband's so-called friends thought about our situation. Specifically, what they thought about me. *Was I the kind of girl who just did not care if the man she shared her life with was out by himself most of the time? And, even if I was not, did I really have any say in the matter? If they knew him, they knew the answer to both questions.*

In his defense, I admit that my husband did spend a little more time at home while I was on bed rest but still not as much as I would have liked. And yet I still held on to the idea that surely he would finally settle down two months later when he became a father.

I soon found out that I was still fooling myself when ten days after our children were born, my cell phone rang at two o'clock in the morning. I was sleeping in the hospital with our son in a crib by my bed and our daughter in the adjoining neonatal intensive care unit room. It is rarely good news when a phone rings in the middle of the night and that call was proof in point.

An emergency room nurse from another hospital an hour away called to tell me that my husband had been in a motorcycle accident. By some grace of God, he was still alive despite having not had a helmet on but his back was hurt in three places.

There were just no words to describe how angry, frustrated and disappointed I was. I thought he was at home in bed curled up with his dogs so he could pick his mother up at the airport bright and early the next morning. She was coming to visit her new grandchildren. Instead, he had been out with his friends and nearly killed himself on the drive home. His children could have grown up having never known their father.

Fortunately, my mother was staying with me in the hospital and had woken up when the phone rang. She volunteered to watch our children while I rushed one hour across town to my husband's bed side.

I could hardly believe my eyes when I first saw him. He was a sight to be seen and while I was thrilled he was alive, I wanted to kill him just the same.

As I sat in a chair at his bedside, all I could think about was that I hoped the accident was a wake-up call but something inside me, feared my hopes were too high. We were still living the nightmare. That behavior had always been who he was and nothing I had ever done or said changed that nor would it have. Change could only come from within him, when and if he was ready.

The events of that evening taught me a lot about my husband. They taught me that the baggage he came with had been a third-party in our relationship since day one and I could not just hope or wish it away. Nothing I had ever done or said changed that nor would it have. Still, I had faith that it could one day be behind him but change would only come from within him; when and if he was ever ready. So, I hung my head and I prayed for strength in my conviction and peace in my heart until that day arrived. The commitment I made was significant enough to me to see where our strange journey was going to take us for I knew our ride had not come to a complete stop.

Chapter 3

As the younger of two children by seven years, I do not recall having baby-sat, changed a diaper, heated up a bottle or burped an infant when I was growing up. As a result, I knew absolutely nothing about babies on the day our children were born. The same held true for my husband.

Knowing very well the ambiguity we were facing when becoming parents, after our children were born, I asked my mother why she did not sit me down during the nine months I was pregnant and tell me what it was like to be a mother.

"Would you have listened to me if I had?" she asked.

I may not have listened to her often in the past but if she had tried to give me advice in that instance, then the answer surprisingly would have been yes. Our two children did not come with an owner's manual, I told her. To that she responded that no child does for no two children are alike.

Although she never said the words, I think my mother was implying that parenthood was something my husband and I had to figure out together. Together, being the operative word. But, as it turned out, it was something I ended up figuring out almost entirely on my own and then teaching my husband.

While watching my mother take the lead on caring for her grandchildren while I was laid up in bed for a week following their birth, I learned how to rock an infant to sleep, how to change a diaper and how to console our babies when they cried. From the hospital nurses in the neonatal intensive care unit, I learned how you bottle-feed, swaddle and bathe them. Collectively, they gave me enough skills so by the time we brought our son and daughter home, I knew just enough to slide by.

It was with the help of a nanny that I survived the first year. She had experience that I did not so she taught me the essential mothering skills, I still did not know. And, while I worked, she taught our children. With her encouragement, they learned to crawl, stand, and then finally to walk. She taught them their first word, how to feed themselves, and how to burp.

It was never in my plan to be a stay-at-home mother so working from home in the room next to where our children were cared for was like having my cake and eating it, too. Admittedly, I did not get a lot of work done given that they wanted to be with me more than they wanted to stay with the nanny so I worked strange hours to meet the demands of both my corporate job and of motherhood.

My husband spent most of his time each day working in his office downstairs. Every time our children reached a new goal, he came upstairs to celebrate. He may have rarely partaken in their development but he was always the gloating father.

This was especially the case when we went on family outings. Our children ate out more often than most of the adults we knew. As a result, they were very well known at the best restaurants in town. They were well behaved and thus drew attention from nearly every patron and half of the wait staff. They enjoyed the attention far more than the food and we enjoyed the opportunities to dine out which was yet another similarity that drew my husband and I together in the first place.

Every time we stopped out as a family, my husband became ever so slightly more drawn in. When there was a diaper to be changed, he took care of it and when one of our children was hungry, he fed them.

Dinners out were the normal family moments that almost made up for all the times it was just the three of us. They were the little glimmers into what I had always known my husband was capable of doing and being and so they kept me hooked like a fish on a line.

On my evenings, I spent home alone with our children, we fine-tuned what they learned during the day. Just by providing them with my undivided attention, I learned how to read our son and daughter without an owner's manual as they showed me what they wanted or needed without saying a word.

When our children were a little over one year old, our nanny moved on. One afternoon, she came into my office and told me that she could no longer work with us. She loved our children to the moon and back but she felt restricted by the fact that I was always ten feet away from them. It made it just too difficult for her to do her job. As happy as I was to save the money I paid her each week, I was paralyzed by the thought that her departure meant that I was about to get a whole lot busier.

For the months that followed, my husband and I did our best to care for our children while we worked. But, the majority of their care, inevitably, fell to me as his job was more demanding and he continued to seek out and take as many opportunities to socialize with his friends as possible.

I must say, I was proud of myself for at least trying to keep up with everything for as long as I did even though it really did not go very well. With the countless number of balls in the air at any given time, I ran around like a mad woman all hours of the day. I was grumpy more often than not and felt as if I could never catch my breath. All thanks to the truth that I was a bit of a perfectionist so I wanted to do everything to the tenth degree. It eventually just became too much.

It took eight months for my husband to see the stress that I was under and admit we needed help. I needed help. At first, we considered hiring another nanny but that was completely just out of the question. The financial burden it placed upon us made it challenging to make the ends meet comfortably each month. It was soon after that sobering reality set in that may husband suggested we move. He was willing to give up the home he loved for us; the same, once glowing mountain home that had for me lost its luster but for him fulfilled a dream.

Moving was our best option for a few reasons. First and foremost, the four of us had outgrown the four walls we shared with six dogs and one cat. Our house was more suitable for a second, weekend home than for a main residence in which to raise children. The isolation that was once a friend had become a foe so we all needed a change of scenery.

Next, since we lived on the top of a mountain, our two public educational options were thirty minutes away either down a winding dirt road or down one of the steepest paved roads in North America. Neither school system had a stellar reputation for providing a record-breaking education so we would have had to invest in two private educations had we stayed in Colorado.

My husband and I also needed to be around other couples our age with children. We needed to surround ourselves with people in the same stage of life as us not those that were single or had decided parenthood was not for them.

Finally, and perhaps most importantly of all, I knew that moving was going to present the only real opportunity for my husband to eventually settle down so I literally and figuratively jumped at the chance.

In a matter of four months, we bought a house in Virginia and sold our house in Colorado. We boxed up our entire life and sent it across country on an eighteen-wheeler. Then, we packed our bags with what little clothes we held behind and readied ourselves for the fourteen-hundred-mile drive across country.

We were a caravan of two. My husband had a trailer to pull and did not trust his SUV to go the distance so he carried his three dogs in a rented SUV while his truck was relocated on a transport. Despite my reservations about my own SUV's ability to make the cross-county drive, a mechanic told me I had no reason for concern so I did not rent an SUV. Instead, we loaded two children, one dog and one cat into my supposedly, road-worthy SUV behind which I pulled a horse trailer to transport my peacock and peahen.

Everything was going just as planned until we reached St. Louis. As we were passing through the city, in the morning rush hour, at seventy miles an hour in the left-hand lane, my left axle snapped like a twig.

I do not recall exactly how the events that followed unfolded, given that I was in a complete state of panic, but I am certain of one thing. While I made a distress call to my husband with one hand, I managed to steer the SUV safely across three lanes of speeding traffic to the next exit with the other. It was not until we all safely made it out of the SUV that we realized how lucky we were to be alive. The left front tire was literally buckled under the frame. To this day, I am certain that the only reason we made it to safety just off the exit for the St. Louis airport rental car agencies where, as luck would have it someone had just returned an SUV, was because a guardian angel had been riding in the passenger seat the whole time.

While my SUV was towed to a car dealer in Virginia, I safely delivered us to Virginia in that rented SUV with our two children, one dog, one cat and two peafowl. The remainder of the trip was so stressful that I drove white-knuckled the entire way while praying that we would make it safely and, when we did, I kissed the ground the moment we arrived.

Given that it was the last day of March and the weather was cold, our furniture delivery was delayed by a week so we spent our first week in Virginia in adjoining rooms in the first hotel we could find that accepted pets. We moved into our new home four months before our children's second birthday.

Chapter 4

There were two factors that drove our decision to move to Virginia rather than to family elsewhere. The first was my ailing father. He had been battling Parkinson's disease for years and had reached the point where it was finally winning. We arrived just in time to share a little more than nine months with him before he passed away.

The second reason was that the county where my family lived just so happened to boast the highest rated elementary school in the state, possibly the country.

My husband attended public school in Oklahoma and I received a private school education in Virginia. We were both college graduates and I held a graduate degree. Since education had always been important to us both, we wanted to place our children in one of the best public-school system in the country.

I thought that moving would be a great change for us all but at first it just turned out to be a great change for me and our children.

I was happy being home after twenty years in Colorado, still it took a little time to get used to being back on the east coast. The idea that that we settled into a house, we had only dreamed of one day calling our own, eased the transition as did the fact that our children finally had their own bedrooms neither of which also served as their playroom. There was more than enough room for us all to spread out.

My husband had never spent any length of time in the eastern part of the county so it was not like anything he had known before. He had spent all of his life in the central and western parts of the country, so the mountains felt like home. Despite his reservations, I remained positive that in time he might start putting down some roots and maybe even grow to like Virginia. Unfortunately, I underestimated how lonely my husband felt after leaving his friends and acquaintances behind and the void it created inside him. So as he struggled with the change, I did what any wife and mother would do. I stepped up to fill the void.

As his wife, I tried to understand what he was going through and to be supportive but I was admittedly not very good at it. I was not very empathetic when I suppose, I should have been, given that I was home with my family and his was still one thousand miles away. It would have made the adjustment a lot easier on us all if I had slowed down long enough to understand.

The preschool years that followed, were exhausting but well worth it given that the bond with our children grew substantially stronger as a result of all my hard work and sacrifice. Our children were already aware enough to know that their mother was always there and so I naturally became the person they turned to for nearly everything. Mom became their favorite new word.

I drove them to preschool nearly every morning and picked them up nearly every afternoon. The only time I did

26

not was when I was traveling or my mother asked to pick them up so they could spend an afternoon together.

I made their breakfasts, packed their lunches and I signed them up for after school activities. While they were in school, I washed and pressed their uniforms. I took off work to attend events like moms and muffins, the thanksgiving feast, the grandparent's day celebration (to which I brought my mother) and international culture day.

I was very involved in what they were studying; very involved. Each afternoon, I asked them what they learned that day in school so they could teach me. I knew what they knew, what they did not know and I worked with them every day to close the gap.

From time to time, my husband would ask our children the same question in our dinner conversation. It seemed as if almost every night they surprised him with how much they knew.

My mother played a very active role over those three years as well. She quickly became such a constant in their lives that they sometimes called her mom and me Omi, a version of the German word for grandmother. She volunteered to read stories to their class and attended all the mother and grandmother events. In fact, my mother was so active at their preschool that the entire staff knew her by name.

My husband was a constant at all of the parent-teacher conferences, made an appearance at one or two thanksgiving lunches and the once a year dads and donuts. After one such event, I asked him if he had met anyone nice, perhaps someone he could befriend. He always just shook his head no and told me the other fathers were kind of nerdy.

I knew him well enough to say that was probably not really the case. Perhaps, it was that they were nothing like the friends he left in Colorado. My hunch was that the fathers were very much about their children and once he was that way himself, he might find that some, definitely not all, were not nearly as nerdy as he thought.

Chapter 5

For two and a half years, our children faithfully attended a Montessori pre-school. They learned, made friends and seemed to enjoy it. We watched them flourish in countless ways until mid-way through their last year. Almost overnight, they no longer had any interest in going to school. Almost overnight, they went from waking up enthusiastic and ready for school to not wanting to get out of bed.

As it turned out, the teacher I thought they adored, the teacher they requested was not the right fit for them. They came to find her teaching style monotonous and not conducive to their needed styles of learning.

You may ask, how two four-years-olds could reach such conclusions and I might have asked so too, had I not had the opportunity to meet the woman myself. We agreed with them wholeheartedly within minutes of meeting with her ourselves. So one more before the end of the school year we agreed that their pre-school education had run its course. We also opted out of enrolling them in the summer program that they had attended the previous two years to let them just enjoy being children for their first summer.

You might next ask yourself, how we could pull two four-year-olds out of pre-school just because they no longer cared for their teacher. The answer was really quite simple. I felt that as their mother, it was my responsibility to make sure they received a quality education without being tormented into developing distaste for school at a very formidable time in their lives. My husband concurred.

It takes a village as they say and having two four-year-olds home for the entire summer was proof in point. It took my mother, my husband, and I working together to make sure their first summer vacation was one to remember.

There were two priorities, I established, for their first summer at home. The first was to prepare them for kindergarten. During orientation, my husband and I were given a packet of information that outlined what our children were expected to know before school started. In it, the expectations were set that they would be able to count to one hundred as well as read and write the alphabet. The education system had certainly come a long way since I was in school given that I did not have such lessons until I was in first grade. My kindergarten was more about art, music and playing.

Each day, whoever watched our children played games to help them learn. Nearly every moment became a learning opportunity. As we drove down the road, we read speed limit signs, bus numbers, license plates and road names. We counted each step we climbed in our house, we sorted the spare change jar and we read books each night. Our children and I played round-robin while counting to one hundred, we sang the alphabet song and they sat on my lap as I typed e-mails.

It amazed me, how much our children grew and matured in those three months and how much I learned about being their mother. I learned that my job was not to just make sure they learned but also to understand how they learned. I came to discover they learned in very different ways.

I came to find that our son was left-brain dominate just like his father. He was very analytical and methodical in his thinking. Because of it, we usually only had to tell him something once. I also came to believe that he had a photographic memory. He never forgot anything and took pride in reminding me when I did.

Conversely, I discovered our daughter was right-brain dominate just like me. She was visual and intuitive so relied on pictures and drawings to help her learn. While she proved herself to be equally as intelligent as her brother, she got far more frustrated when learning than he did.

The second priority of their summer vacation was to have fun. That was where my husband really got involved. He bought our children a classic video game console that housed all the games we used to play as teenagers – Frogger, Packman, Donkey Kong, you name it. When he first brought it home, I honestly thought it was more for him than for our children but over time they came to enjoy it as much as he did. Although it cost a small fortune, it more than paid for itself in hours of family fun.

My husband also purchased a dirt bike for our son and then orchestrated the family purchase of two four-wheelers for their fifth birthday. Later, he bought one for himself so he could ride alongside our son while our daughter's collected dust in the barn. She was a little too small to ride so hers sat idle in the garage until she was ready to ride it.

For my version of summer fun, we painted pictures, colored in coloring books and put together jigsaw puzzles. We built a fort in the bedroom, covered it in blankets, surrounded it with pillows and then crawled inside for a nap. Next, we painted our faces and played dressed up in old Halloween costumes. Each day, our daughter transformed herself into a Disney princess and our son became a Marvel superhero. Our daughter also began teaching herself to play guitar, which I used to play, while our son began teaching himself to play the saxophone, which my husband used to play. They would invite us to their shows where they performed duets while singing into the karaoke microphones.

It was certainly an action-packed summer but I bet our children would say that their favorite part was going to the pool once or twice a week with their Omi.

My mother lived in a small gated-community with a pool that was perfect for toddlers to practice all of their swimming skills. In a matter of three months, they transitioned from life-vests to noodles. They did hand stands in the shallow end of the pool, swam from end-to-end and even learned how to dive. By the time the pool closed on Labor Day weekend, I was certain they had grown gills.

With each passing day, our children developed into what I referred to as real little people. Their personalities grew as large as their vocabularies. They became opinionated, outspoken, self-confident and comical. As such, they gave us our first glimpse into the people they would soon become.

When it came to our son, my husband was about as involved as he could have been. It made sense that since it was easier for him to identify with our son and partake in boy activities; that was where he spent the majority of his free time. Our son very much enjoyed riding his dirt bike or the four-wheeler with his father, walking the dogs, working on cars and riding the tractor.

Fortunately for my husband, our son was sweeter than a plate of chocolate cookies. He was loving, adoring and forgiving. When my husband stepped out of line and apologized, my son always accepted his apology. He held no grudges which my husband needed. I did not hold grudges anymore either but I did not forget as easily.

My husband was less apt at dealing with our daughter. He clearly adored her but it was also quite clear that they were cut from the same stone. It was crustal clear that she, too, was fiercely independent, had no problem speaking her mind and marched to the beat of her own drum. The two of them clashed heads all summer long as each stood firm in their place of trying to impose their will on the other. It was a scene to watch.

I contributed my husband's lack of patience and his need for occasional separation from our daughter as a direct result of having grown up as an only child (for all intents and purposes) and for not having a sister around from which to learn. Fortunately, my son is growing up with a sister. I believe that because of it, he is a chivalrous and considerate, true southern gentlemen.

The summer could not have come to an end soon enough. Our son was hungry to go out into the world to really start learning and our daughter was ready to make

33

new friends. I was ready for the world to finally find out what amazing children we had and for my husband to return to his work-school routine which I believe he secretly missed. He was, too.

At the same time, I wondered what the next chapter in our lives held in store for me. In some respects, I suspected, it would be easier than the last three-years because I no longer had to drive our children back and forth to pre-school or wash their uniforms every day. But I also suspected it would be more challenging because a whole new set of responsibilities was coming my way. I honestly had no idea what to expect from kindergarten and neither did my husband for that matter.

Just as school was about to start, I appreciated that my husband was deeper into his roles of husband and father. In all fairness, I do believe that he caught up with my expectations as much as he could but his abilities still did not line up. That being the case, I decided that I needed to step up my game even further and so I did.

Chapter 6

I had started to come to terms with the idea that my husband was not going to just settle down anytime soon so I spent the summer months focused on one course of action. All I wanted to do was transform myself into a strong and courageous woman with a confident voice from a lost in translation, middle-aged mother of two.

After fifteen personal improvements, I was ready to single-handedly fill the parenting roles for as long as needed better than I had ever done before.

Of all the enhancements I made, there were three that proved the most beneficial.

First, I revamped my eating habits. By following the Mediterranean diet, I lost ten pounds and found hourglass curves, I had never seen before. I had the energy, I needed to keep up with all of the additional demands that were placed upon me and I physically looked better than I had in a decade. The latter was very important to me because I wanted our children to be proud to introduce me to all of their new friends and I was going to be making a lot of first impressions.

This change altered my personal perception immensely. When I looked good, I naturally had more confidence and with that came the courage I needed to make the decisions and call the shots for our children and for me. When I felt frumpy, I had little confidence so I was insecure about making decisions. This change really drove home the idea of looking and dressing the part.

Next, I harnessed my messy mind. Being a mother of five-year-old twins required me to wear many hats at once. To do so, meant, I had to be organized, focused, and resourceful. Suddenly, I was drinking from a water hose with the countless new demands placed upon me so I had to stay focused. Through the art of mindfulness, I learned how to stop long enough to rate each task to decide how best to spend my time.

By becoming mindful, I was constantly aware of what was really important, of my priorities and of my needs versus wants. I was able to focus on and rise to the occasions that mattered.

For years, time ran away from me and I always felt as if there just was not enough of it. I constantly longed for more hours in the day. But that ended when mindfulness helped me to work smarter not harder. Suddenly, I had more than enough time in the day for everything. A point I desperately needed to reach given that I was about to really start orchestrating not only my life but also the lives of our children.

The third significant lifestyle change I made was to speak up.

When my husband and I got together, I was a much stronger woman than I was after we married and especially after we had children. Being single, forced me to become such. But, since my husband had a very strong voice, mine had dulled over the years.

To become mine and our children's advocate, I had to be firm in my convictions and loud in my voice. I had to be a take-charge kind of woman capable of running the show and stepping up to the plate when necessary. I had to be confident and courageous in my decision-making and call the shots even when I was not up to the task. I had to set schedules and makes meetings, doctor's appointments and dentist appointments. And, I had to do it every single day because that was who our children counted on me to be.

Fortunately, I had never had an issue speaking up in my professional life so I already had that persona inside me. All I had to do was transition it to my personal life.

When my transformation was complete, I was in the right physical and mental state of mind to not only take care of our children but to also better take care of myself.

Our son once told me, he came down from heaven to take care of me. I found that a rather curious statement especially coming from a child who knew little to nothing about God and heaven. Still, it had merit in that, before my transformation, I had no clear sense of direction in my life and was on my way to becoming a complete stranger to myself. Our son gave me the reason and courage, I needed to turn my life around.

He was looking to my husband and me for guidance on how to continue developing into a true southern gentleman so to be his mother I had to be responsible and accountable. As luck would have it, he was naturally chivalrous, considerate and helpful without being asked. He believed in ladies first, carried my purse for me, and helped out with his sister. He was the little boy whom all of the other little boys in his class wanted to call friend and on whom the giddy little girls had a crush.

Our daughter had an independent and stubborn streak, a mile-wide so she looked to me to teach her how to make those characteristics constructive and not destructive. She had very strong opinions – just like her father – and spoke half the time without thinking first. Also, just like her father. She was the little girl that drew you in like puppy dogs and babies. Once you looked into those big, green eyes you were forever changed.

There was no doubt in my mind that our daughter came down from heaven to help me take life a little less seriously. Because of her free spirit, she sang as if no one was listening and danced as if no one was watching. She cracked jokes, laughed at herself, and even cried if the spirit moves her. To be her mother, I had to be silly, carefree, and funny.

I believed that our children needed not worry about anything other than being five years old. They had no need to worry about when it was time to go to the doctor once a year or to the dentist twice a year. They had no concern about what time the school bus picked them up or what time it brought them home. And, it was none of their concern whether there was food on the table or clothes on their backs. I wish, I could have said that for all the little boys and girls in the world their age.

While I was writing this chapter, I took our children to a pool party. Once the twenty wild children entered the pool, I sat in a chair just outside a glass door to chat with the other mothers who were spending their Saturday afternoon at a child's birthday party. In the middle of our conversation, I watched our daughter leave the pool and then push the over-sized glass door next to me open with all her strength. All the mothers stopped talking and turned their heads in her direction. Next, the most unexpected thing happened.

"Mommy, I love you," my daughter said.

I smiled for my heart was instantly full.

"I love you too, baby," I replied.

She gave me a dripping wet hug and kiss then, as quickly as she appeared, she was gone.

Every mother placed her hand over her heart and awed at my daughter. They could not stop telling me how lucky I was and how sweet my daughter was (both of which I already knew). They also went on to say that they would have given anything in the world to have their daughters or sons say those three little words to them without their having to say them first. It was validation, I was doing a good job of being their mother.

After we returned to our conversation, I overheard one mother ask another where her husband was to which she replied that he was at home watching television. It was clear by the expressions on all of the women's faces that their husbands, too, had no interest in attending a children's birthday party on a Saturday afternoon just as mine had not either.

On the way home, our son could not thank me enough for taking him to the party. He went on and on about how much fun he had and it was clear from the smile on his face that his every word was the truth. He, too, told me he loved me.

I listened as our children talked about what they enjoyed most that afternoon and shared the candy that they had received in their goody bags. They rambled on the entire drive to the pizza parlor and then on to our house.

It was just the three of us and it felt good. It felt right. I realized that it was the most normal we had ever known and maybe there had never been anything wrong with that after all. There once was a time, when I was preoccupied with the fact that my husband was missing in action, as I had heard another mother earlier that evening put it, but those days were behind me. I had finally moved past the need to mope around. There was no reason to spend the energy in such a useless way any longer.

We returned home to find my husband sitting at the breakfast bar waiting on his pizza. Once our son joined him, he asked him if he had a good time, to which our son responded that he had. Our daughter agreed. I was sure that was clear from the pictures I had sent him earlier in the evening but I still appreciated the fact that he asked.

As a working mother of five-year-old twins, I had split responsibilities. On one hand, I had a job that paid the bills and a salary that worked with my husband to make our world go around. I was raised to become a successful, career woman and it was as much a part of me as my auburn hair and freckles. It was not as much about what I was as it was about who I was.

As a project manager, I was responsible for up to six projects at any given time which requires me to operate at a highly organized and communicative level of excellence.

My employer counted on me as did my customers. To my good fortune, my corporate job was the perfect companion and commitment to my role as a wife and mother.

On the other hand, my husband needed a supportive partner while he figured out how to wrestle and contain his drive to be social. He needed a sounding board, a friend, and a support system. Despite his inability to deliver my white picket fence, fairy tale dream in any other way other than by his own means and according to his schedule, he had a good heart, a strong sense of humor, and he cared for others to a fault. And, I loved him.

As I watched my husband and son's pizza party, I found peace in the idea that our state of affairs was far more normal than abnormal based on the number of mothers alone at the party. And, I had a full heart because our children were happy, they loved me and they knew I loved them. In that moment, I let my dream of the fairy tale family go. I let go of the dream of the white picket fence, the family vacations and the pictures in front of the fireplace for Christmas cards. And, I finally accepted that fairy tales were all just smoke and mirrors just like the idea of perfection.

Chapter 7

The two most predictable events of my weekday mornings were that our children went to school and I went to work. Other than that, anything and everything about how we reach those two outcomes was as uncertain as a deck of cards stacked on a table that could have fallen at any time.

If our daughter stayed up past eight o'clock the night before, the chances were that she slept in. But, if she fell asleep before seven o'clock, I heard the pitter-patter of her tiny feet in the hallway before the rooster down the road crowed the dawn of the new day.

Sometime around six o'clock in the morning, my daughter – Morning Glory as I nicknamed her – came into our room and woke me. She had no regard for the time displayed on her bedroom clock when she decided she was ready to start her day. And, she had no regard for the fact that I was still sleeping when she tapped me on the shoulder – tap, tap, tap – until I woke up. It seemed no matter how deep my sleep.

Occasionally, I sent her back to her room to watch television until I was ready to get up then other times I invited her to lie in bed next to me. But, more often than not, I accommodated her request and simply just got out of

42

bed because that gave me the opportunity for some one-on-one time with her that I may not have otherwise gotten in the day.

It went without saying that she was hungry the moment she woke up so while I brewed a pot of coffee, her plate of eight pancakes cooked in the microwave. We both knew, I was never alert enough to keep up with her conversation that started the moment she opened her eyes and her feet hit the ground until I had my first cup of coffee.

Around half past the hour, my husband finally found his way downstairs to let his dogs out. As he passed us by, he said good morning before shuffling down the hall to his office to log into his work computer. He returned to the kitchen ten minutes later to find his first cup of coffee sitting next to his computer at his kitchen desk. He was a man of few words until he, too, drank his first cup of coffee.

While our daughter and I talked, she ate her pancakes and my husband read the latest news snippets aloud. He spat out headlines and statistics that I neither could focus on nor cared about at the moment. It was no surprise then that when he asked my opinion, I returned little to no intelligent response. Still, the dialogue carried on as I juggled two conversations.

If our son was not awake by the time she finished her pancakes, I asked her to run upstairs to wake him. He had thirty minutes to clear the cobwebs from a deep night's sleep and make it to the bus stop on time.

Our son was a night owl. Despite all my best efforts to wear him out throughout the evening, he usually sat up with my husband and me watching television far past a respectable bedtime. His excuse was that he could not go to sleep until I went to sleep. He reminded each evening that it was his job to watch over me after all.

I was usually tired when it came to sitting up with our son but I still welcomed the time together. He lay with his head on my shoulder while we watched television until he could no longer keep his little eyes open. It was the perfect way to end my day.

There are some people in the world that pop right up in the morning but our son was not one of them. He was as slow to rise as he was to go to sleep. But once he was finally awake, he typically made his way directly to the couch to watch cartoons while his sister disappeared into the sunroom to play a round of video games.

While my husband fed the dogs, I prepared lunches. When they started school, our children were so excited about eating in the cafeteria. In about two weeks, they discovered that the food was not nearly as good as that which I packed so they boycotted buying lunch. The cafeteria was certainly much easier for me but I did agree it was just not the same a lunch packed with mommy love.

When I traveled, my husband stepped in but, from what I understood, he did not do things the way I did. He did not cut the crust off the bread despite our daughter explaining to him that was the way mommy did it nor did he slip one piece of candy into the lunch boxes. He packed a healthy lunch while I packed a balanced lunch, which included at least one lovingly selected piece of candy that left them thinking about me throughout the afternoon hours.

By that time, it was straight up at the seven o'clock hour, my morning was actually, just getting interesting.

Before our daughter made her way downstairs for breakfast, she dressed for the day and brushed her hair. She was ready to go to school.

Her brother, however, still asked me to help him dress. It was not that he could not do it himself, I think he just liked the idea that I picked out his clothes. Once he was dressed, he joined his sister in the bathroom to brush their teeth and comb their hair while I hastily scurried down the hall to my closet to change into sweatpants and a sweatshirt. Minutes later we met at the top of the stairs.

If the plan was to ride the bus, we took a sharp right turn at the bottom of the stairs which meant I drove them the mile down the road to the bus stop. The next fifteen minutes passed at a breakneck speed.

First, I helped our son with his socks and shoes then our daughter with just her shoes. Next, I packed their backpacks – school folders, lunch boxes, and water bottles – while they hunted down their coats, gloves, and hats depending on the weather. Then, they added whatever little trinkets they decided to share with their friends to the secret compartments of their backpacks just before they walked out the door.

Our son was not much of a breakfast eater especially on the days he raced out the door to the bus stop so he would skip his customary bowl of cereal and head straight out to the car. His sister quickly followed.

If the plan was for me to drop them off at school, we took a relaxed left at the bottom of stairs which meant I drove our children the mile down the road so the next thirty minutes were relaxed.

Since their elementary school opened twenty minutes after the bus was scheduled to pick them up, there was more than enough time for our son to eat breakfast – a bowl of Lucky Charms cereal – which he enjoyed while watching Sponge Bob Square Pants on the kitchen television. Afterward, he met his dad in the sunroom for a quick round of video games.

If my husband kissed our children on their way out the door, I knew he did not have time for the five-minute ride to the bus stop or school. But, if he poured himself a second cup of coffee, we waited patiently for him to join us in the car.

At either drop-off point, the first chapter of my weekday mornings closed with our son and daughter giving me, or us, a kiss and hug goodbye. That made all the work each morning more than worth my effort.

By the time the school bell rang, I was already back home. I was tired but my day was just getting started. There were breakfast dishes to clear and the kitchen to return to working order from the craziness of the morning before I checked in at my other full-time job. All of which I took care of while sipping my second cup of coffee.

I once asked my husband to help in the mornings and he did so for about one week. He saw all of the work that went into getting our children out the door each morning and said he was available to help out. And yet, the only time he stepped in was when I was out of town. Perhaps he resolved that sitting in the kitchen with us counted as help or that he was technically already at work given that he had logged into his computer regardless of the fact that his office was a ten-second walk down the hall.

For whatever excuse he created, the situation was really, quite simple. In my opinion, he could have helped out given that he had plenty of time to perform all of his routine internet searches and to play video games. The time he could have used to help them get dressed, brush their teeth and put on their coats.

There was once a time in my life when his lack of participation would have bothered the hell out of me but those days had passed. I learned to just let it go and stop asking him for help. Our children did, too. Instead, they just came directly to me for support and I happily gave it to them. My morning routine was to get them to school on the best note possible and that was exactly what I did.

Chapter 8

When our children went to school, I went to my corporate job. I was one of the seven-in-ten mothers in the workforce and that had always been the case. Fortunately, I worked for a company that puts family first and completely understood the demands placed on the modern-day mother.

As a project manager in corporate America, it was my responsibility to keep track of the schedule and expenditures for each of my projects while I drove to a timely and successful conclusion. In other words, I spent my days managing money and checking items of a project plan until all the work was complete.

In my personal life, I did the exact, same thing, day in and a day out just but I went by a different title – wife or mother. I grocery shopped, cooked, cleaned, set schedules and chauffeured our children around town all in the interest of giving them the best childhood experience possible.

Take laundry, for instance. It never ceased to amaze me how much laundry two little people could create.

Our son, typically wore an outfit one time (something my husband used to as well). As a boy's boy, he was always into something and got dirty because of it. Either he had stains on his shirt or dirt on his knees. So every time he changed, his clothes went directly into the laundry room.

His sister changed clothes two to three times a day. After which her clothes rarely made their way to the laundry rooms she constantly lost track of what was clean and what was dirty. So, she either left her clothes in piles on the floor or hid them under her bed. By the time I found them, I could not make heads or tails of what was clean or dirty myself so by default, everything ended up in the dirty clothes hamper, too.

After I put the first load of laundry into the washing machine, I logged into my computer to check and see how many meetings, I had been invited to and how many emails were waiting for a response. That painted a mental picture of how I would alternate between my two full-time jobs for the few hours our children were in school.

Once I had my mind wrapped around the cadence of my day, the first thing I did was reset my house. Resetting my house meant that I returned any items our children had played with the night before to their rightful place in the house. Some days, I ran around for minutes and some days, I ran around for an hour. It all depended on how much my family cooperated when I asked them to pick up after themselves.

I hated the clutter. It stifled my mind and restricted my breathing. I felt weighed-down when surrounded by it so having two children who left little trails behind them wherever they went was very challenging for me. I constantly picked up after them because I had no intention of living in an untidy home.

Once the clutter was dissipated, I spent some time doing something nice for myself.

There was a time in my life when our children defined me, which meant I spent most, if not all of my time, doing motherly things. I was so consumed in our children's lives and their reflection on me that I lost track entirely of myself.

When I first lost my job nine-months after relocating to Virginia, I had too much time on my hands. I went from a working mother to a stay-at-home mother which did not suit me at all. That was when I came up with the idea to start a blog. I knew I was not the only middle-aged mother in the midst of a life change so I start a blog to offer support and give inspiration as I sought and found answers. I envisioned it as a place where women could come together and do the same. I had grand ideas but I just could not get them off the ground. I shut my blog down two months later.

In the little time I took for myself each day, I wrote. I spent one hour a day, usually at lunch, writing a chapter in my latest book. When I began the journey to become an author, I ambitiously wrote two of the three books of the Suzanne Style's trilogy. I self-published both books with little success so I decided to redirect my talents into something a little more me.

The idea of helping women navigate the twisted waters of motherhood continued to haunt me after I put the idea of a blog to rest so I chronicled my transformation and how it changed my life in what became my first attempt at writing non-fiction. It came naturally to me so I decided that writing non-fiction was my calling. If my writing inspired at least one woman then my career as an author was validated. That one hour a day I spent writing about my life and my experiences made me feel as if, even with all of my roles and responsibilities, I was finally moving in the direction of reaching my goal to one day leave corporate America behind me as I achieved the status of Best-Selling Author.

For the rest of the time, our children were in school, I scheduled a doctor's appointment and playdates. I signed them up for after school activities like girl scouts, soccer, and dance. And, I straightened up their rooms.

When the minutes ticked down to less than an hour before our children returned home, I took one last inventory of my unfinished chores for the day. Perhaps, it was putting away the last load of laundry I managed to wash, cleaning the litter box or vacuuming. And, just for fun, I prepared a surprise for them if I had one. They were always so excited to see me that I liked to do something extra special for them.

By the time I picked our children up either from the bus stop or from school, I was certainly more rested than I was when I dropped them off which was fortunate since I was then only half-way through my day. The dynamics of my recently quiet house drastically changed and everyone began talking over one another, the dogs barked and the cats meowed. All the lights went on and the video game console played its familiar tunes. But, most important of all, the marathon of little people calling for me was once again underway. As much as it frustrated me, I would not have had it any other way.

Chapter 9

By three o'clock each weekday afternoon, our children were home from school. The third part of my day was underway which meant I had to balance two more hours of work while watching our children. Fortunately, we had fallen into somewhat of a routine that carried us into the evening hours.

The very first thing our children did every afternoon when they got home from school was, hang their coats, and backpacks in the hallway closet then set their shoes in the rack below. From there, they went straight to the pantry for a snack. They were starving or so they told me. They could eat anything within reach as long as they followed my one simple rule – for each healthy snack they ate, they could have one unhealthy snack.

My daughter loved mandarin oranges so I could count on that being her healthy snack. She learned to peel the orange herself and place it in a bowl. Our son loved apples so I cut one into handheld sections which he then placed into a bowl. They sat together for about five minutes watching cartoons, which translated into five minutes for me to fire off one or two more emails before the next round of eating.

Next, they helped themselves to one unhealthy snack. Ice cream was about the only unhealthy snack our children could agree upon so chances were they shared in an ice cream party. It was not unusual for either my husband or me, sometimes even both of us, to join in.

That was when the real fun began. It never failed to amaze me how our children got so hyped-up on sugar. It was as if a force took over and they had an out-of-body experience. I got tired just watching them.

For the next hour, our son and daughter ran circles around the house and each other. They got into anything and everything and no matter what my husband or I said; it all fell on deaf ears.

My husband played with our children for the first thirty minutes they were home, but when they transformed into little monsters, he disappeared back into his office. That was my queue to lay them down in their rooms to rest. While our daughter napped, our son watched his favorite cartoon.

As strange as it may sound, that was the first real hour of the day that I sat still. I did not have someone calling mommy every five seconds, my husband asking me some questions or another and my chores for the day were the better part of done. So, with a dog at my feet and my two cats basking in the late afternoon sun next to my desk, I took seven slow, deep breaths to recharge my batteries.

It may also sound strange but I had my greatest moments of comfort during that hour. I found peace in knowing that our children were safely home and that their stomachs were full. I found comfort in knowing, they were a little smarter, a little more outgoing and that they spent their day playing with friends. Not to mention that my workday would come to an end soon so I could return to doing that I loved the most – being a wife and a mother.

When my workday finally came to an end, my first order of business was cooking dinner.

In our house, dinner was a social event. After everyone gathered in the kitchen, my husband executed his evening internet search routine at the kitchen desk while our children took up residency on the bar stools. And while the television in the corner aired the evening news, our dogs laid on their beds just off to the side in the family room. Even a cat or two snuck downstairs to sit on the stairs to investigate why everyone had gathered together.

I imagine that our children were like most children their age when it came to their eating habits. They had their staple foods, they enjoyed such as chicken nuggets, buttered noodles, and pizza. On occasion, they did venture out into soft tacos but only when I made up a special batch at home. And, they even ventured out to eat a hot dog from time to time.

While I prepared dinner, I also set the table. If the four of us ate together, we sat at the kitchen table. But, if it was just three of us, ate at the breakfast bar. There was something more intimate about our meal when the three sat side-by-side and talked about their day. Or, we watched their favorite cartoons, ones they had probably seen a dozen or more times. The only nights on which I did not cook dinner was when we had an engagement, like dance, soccer, or a social club meeting.

After everyone excused themselves from the table, I cleaned the kitchen while our children ate dessert or played their last video games of the night. If my husband was home, he joined our children in the sunroom. By the time I turned off the lights in the kitchen for the night, a victor had been declared.

When I was growing up, we had a family pact that the person who cooked dinner never cleaned the kitchen after dinner since there were two adults in the house. I dropped that hint to my husband several times and yet I still ended up doing both. For the longest time I complained about it but when we reached a point where everyone brought their dirty dishes to the sink, I figured what was the point. I took my little win and moved on.

After the lights downstairs went out, my husband retired upstairs to take his evening bath before going to bed while I sat down with our children to do their homework. After which they took their baths, dried their hair and brushed their teeth. A bedtime story followed. In our home, every night was a two-story night; one my son selected and the other my daughter. It seemed that only on rare occasions one of them chose a book that they agreed upon. Regardless of whether or not they nodded-off by the time story-time ended, I tucked them into bed with a kiss good night.

By the time I shuffled my way down the hall to our bedroom, my husband was already lying in bed watching one of his favorite shows. So, I took the opportunity for some more me time. Maybe it was to read a magazine, perhaps to write another chapter in my latest book, to catch up on Hollywood gossip or even play a game on my iPad. Whatever I chose, it was just one more little opportunity to do and have something that was entirely my own.

The dogs were already asleep and the cats had made their way into their favorite blanket in some dark corner of a quiet bedroom. That was one of my favorite times of the day because my family was content in their beds yawning and stretching. It was confirmation that the home I worked so hard to create made my loved ones feel warm, safe, and loved.

As sure as the moon hung high in the sky, one of our children came asking for a bedtime snack. The second child always followed. While I tried not to make eating before going to bed a habit, when our children came to tell me they were hungry, I had no choice but to answer their call. Dinner had long since passed and breakfast was too far away to think about so inevitably they needed something to carry them through the night.

If it was only my dog sleeping upstairs, then our late-night picnic took place at the coffee table in the master bedroom after which we all crawled into bed. I waited for them to fall deeply asleep before carrying them to bed where I tucked them in with traditional hug and kiss on the forehead before whispering, I love you, in their ears.

Our son told me that he had a dream once in which I disappeared in the middle of the night and he was not able to find me when he woke up. Since then, on most night nights he got up and crawled in bed with me about thirty minutes later. His sister followed suit for she simply did not want to sleep at the other end of the house all alone. At that point, I volunteered to sleep in the guest room with our children.

After a brief deliberation (which I always seemed to lose) about who would be sleeping in the middle, we crawled in bed and turned out the lights to talk.

I loved our late-night talks. As the moon shined through the bedroom window, there was a soft glow on their faces. They shared with me what they were studying in school, who they played with, who was nice, who was mean and what was their favorite part of the day. From those conversations, I learned where I needed to concentrate my efforts as their mother.

By nine o'clock in the evening, I was both physically and mentally exhausted. I had run my errands, cleaned the house, done the laundry, cooked the meals, cleaned the kitchen, and put in a full day of work at the office. And, I had still found the energy to feed the cats and birds, return my personal emails, pay some bills, and prepare myself to do it all over again the next day.

When our children were fast asleep and my dog was snoring on the floor beside the bed while one cat lay curled up beside my leg, I said my good night prayers. I thanked the Lord above for the wonderful life he had given me and for my wonderful family. I thanked Him for the grace and fortitude to carry on each day and asked for the strength to always be the best wife and mother ever.

Chapter 10

There was a sense of relief that came with the weekend in that I had one less full-time job that required my attention. My focus was one hundred percent on my children, my husband, our home, and on me. That did not mean that I was any less busy, it just meant that I was busier with the things in life that mattered the most.

My weekday mornings were so hectic that I preferred to start the weekends on a low note. We set no alarm; there were no plans to follow and no schedules to keep unless otherwise unavoidable. And, even then, I waited as late on Saturday morning as possible to schedule us to be anywhere.

Saturday morning was about a big family breakfast. After I brewed my daily pot of coffee, I fried up a pound of bacon or a package of link sausages. If our daughter and I were lucky and moved fast enough, we could stake claim to a piece or two before the plate was emptied in the blink of an eye. A plate of pancakes followed for her and scrambled eggs with plenty of cheese for the rest of us. Any leftovers and there were intentionally always leftovers, became a morning snack for the dogs.

There was something very mothering about preparing a hearty breakfast for my family. Especially one that I knew they would enjoy even though we rarely sat down together to eat it. We ate on a first-come, first-served basis until nothing remained of the bacon plate but a grease-stained paper towel and the egg pan had been wiped clean. Then, as quickly as my family gathered, they disappeared but I still heard them in the background as I poured myself a second cup of coffee to sip on while I cleaned the dishes.

My son, most likely, played video games with his father so he ran in and out of the kitchen when it was his opponent's turn to make sure I was still there, while my daughter sat on the family room couch watching cartoons. I watched one of my silly reality shows in the kitchen that I recorded, who knew when. I had shows that I liked to watch but I never knew when they aired nor would I have time to watch them even if I had.

When the lunch hour arrived sooner than expected, (and it always did), we were finally ready to contemplate leaving the house. My husband found the structure of our weekday mornings far too hectic so his long-standing ask was that the weekends be less structured. I agreed, however, I also knew that our children had needs and wants that I did not have time to address during my workweek so I inevitably had weekend errands to run. It was not that my husband did not understand, it was that he was of the opinion that children can make shopping stressful and overwhelming. I agreed, still, that did not change the facts.

While my husband disappeared into our bedroom to get ready, I disappeared into our children's rooms. It was still my responsibility to get them dressed, do their hair and help

59

them brush their teeth even on the weekends. They knew no difference in my role given the day of the week. I was still waiting for the day to come when my son realized he knew how to dress himself.

Once the three of them were ready and had returned downstairs, it was finally my turn to get dressed. I always thought I had more than enough time to get ready until our children started checking on my progress and my husband yelled up the stairs that he was ready to go. Given that I hated being rushed, I could have become irritated and snappy from the pressure or just let it go and move on. In the interest of having a pleasant day together, I always opted for the latter.

It rarely failed that once we left the house, our children nodded off before we reached the highway. While it thrilled me that they were taking a nap given that my little morning-glory was up again before the sun, they threw an instant wrench in any plans we made.

If we were out to run errands and eat lunch, then my husband and I took turns running into the stores depending on whose stop it was. That delayed the inevitable of waking our son and our daughter as long as possible. If we were just out for lunch, we took a leisurely drive to the farthest destination we could set, again, delaying the inevitable.

No matter what our Saturday brought, it would inevitably include a certain chain of events.

To start, our children would argue with us about leaving the house in the first place. They always preferred to be home. It was typically my husband's idea to go out as he reminded us that he had spent the entire week cooped up working from home.

Next, our children would inevitably get tired of being away from home if we were out for too long. Depending on how much fun my husband was having, I would cave sooner than him and recommend we called it an afternoon. Then again, he could have surprised us and called it an afternoon first. It really just all depended on whether or not he felt as if he was actually having his weekend experience.

Once we had safely returned home, we would finally come together to agree that was no place like home, which was the reason our children did not want to leave in the first place. So, we once again locked the world outside when the door closed behind us.

I went back to work once everyone was settled. I was arguably not very good at sitting down and relaxing because I could not sit still for any length of time when I knew there were still chores to be done. Perhaps, it was a stack of ironing or mopping the kitchen floor. Most likely, I had forgotten to water my plants during the week and my bird's aviary needed attention. Or, depending on the time of year, the garden needed watering or the landscape had been overrun with weeds.

It no longer astonished me that I could just walk around our home and see work that no one else saw. Perhaps they chose not to see anything because they knew that I would get around to this or that eventually despite the fact that my plate was full raising two children, working a full-time job, and trying to have a life of my own.

Before I knew it, dinnertime was upon us so I found myself back in the kitchen cooking and cleaning, again. Fortunately, I could work myself in and back out of the kitchen early enough in the evening that I had a few hours before bedtime to let my hair down. Sometimes, I built a Lego's tower with our son or played hair salon and makeup artist with our daughter. Whatever it was, that was my time to have fun and be silly.

No matter how my day went, Saturday nights typically came to the same close. In whatever way we got there, the four of us laid snuggled together in the king-size bed watching television. Our daughter fell asleep first and our son followed suit about one hour later. My husband usually fell asleep at about the same time as our daughter.

After I finished watching whatever program for whatever reason was still playing on the television, I carried my daughter to bed and tucked her in with a kiss on the check and I love you whispered in her ear. She was still small enough that I could carry her down the hall to her bedroom without hurting my back. I wish I could have said the same about her brother. He was approaching nearly half my weight and was already two-third as tall as me. Still, I never missed the chance to tuck him in so, after I struggled to get him into my arms, we shuffled down the hall to his room where I tucked him in the same way.

Before returning to bed, I stopped to kiss my dog goodnight and give her a belly scratch as I told her she was the best dog in the world. I fluffed my pillow and then crawled under a mound of blankets regardless of the time of year.

Without fail, just as I was about to kiss my husband good night, he woke up and asked for his nightly head rub. I begrudgingly agreed even though it only lasted a few minutes for I was ready to go to sleep myself. It was never the act of rubbing his head that irritated me, it was his timing. It stunk.

Eventually, I finally faded off into my well-earned rest where I stayed until I heard the pitter-patter of our daughter's little feet coming down the hallway in the wee hours of the morning.

Chapter 11

Sundays were our established day of rest. After six full days of being on the go, my mind and body needed time to rejuvenate before the madness of a new week began. And, fortunately, my family agreed thus we only ever have two standing plans for any given Sunday.

Our first scheduled activity was to attend church.

In her childhood, my mother was a very devout Catholic and so my parents decided that my brother and I would follow suit. I lived by their decision until I turned eighteen and graduated from high school. It was then that I made the decision to stop practicing Catholicism for various personal reasons and I had never gone back.

I did not, however, stop believing in God. I had always been a firm believer. I had faith in a force much greater than myself. God was a force from which my dreams were born and the universe was the energy that molded them into reality. Faith in them both turned my thoughts into reality and rewarded me for living a responsible, considerate, and kind life.

My husband was a Baptist when he was a child. When we first got together, I never knew him to go to church or to really pray but his mother was a devout Christian and that was what I have watched him since become. Once he was transformed, it became important to him that our children welcomed God into their lives as well. He showed them the way by being baptized two years ago. He, too, was a true believer.

About one year ago, we found our way to a local community bible-based church. It was only after we tried two other churches in our area that we came to settle into what we now consider our worshipping family. While my husband and I attended the big church (as our children called it) they attended the little church or bible study. Or, on the Sundays when we just did not feel like leaving the house, we watched a live broadcast of the sermon on the internet in our pajamas.

Seeing that the family went to church was my husband's single clearest attempt to be the active leader of our family. It was his committed time to not go out and be social but rather to build and strengthen the bonds that tied with his wife, children, and God. Watching him do that week after week showed me that he was far more capable of giving himself to his family and his faith than he demonstrated. And, whether he saw it that way or not, he had taken a crucial step towards settling down.

I, too, was very committed to my faith but I did not feel the need to go to church every week in the demonstration. I believed that God heard my voice and read my thoughts wherever I was and whatever I was doing. He was all listening and all-knowing. I also believed the universe's energy never slept.

Still, I went to church every Sunday because it was important enough to my husband that our children learn about God through church and it was important to me that I supported this move on his part. It was, after all, I had been waiting on that sign for five years.

Sometimes after church, my husband liked to go out for lunch but our children and I preferred to spend the rest of the day at home especially during football season.

For nearly all the years that my husband and I had been together, we played fantasy football. It was as intricate to our relationship as was our love of animals. So, it went without saying that we spent Sunday afternoons watching football and, of course, snacking. Every time I turned around, I found someone standing in the pantry looking for something to eat including myself. That behavior just came naturally to some of my family as did napping.

While my husband and daughter napped on and off, my son and I played with his toys while watching the games. We built Lego towers, raced matchbox cars or played video games. My son had a great imagination so I enjoyed following his lead in games of make-believe.

If there was any day of the week that I could get away with not cooking dinner, Sunday was it. After my family spent the better part of five to six hours grazing their way through the pantry and the refrigerator, they did not want a sit-down dinner. Any remaining leftovers from the week served us quite well and gave us the full stomachs we needed to send ourselves to bed.

The last waking hours of Sunday evening were an exact replica of the evening before. In fact, the only nights that I did not tuck our children in were when I was traveling or they spent the night with my mother. My husband knew how much it meant to me to do this ritual for as long as I could carry our children. Besides, something in me believed that they knew it is me who carried them to bed, kissed them good night, and whispered in their ears.

Regardless of how we spent the weekend, it was all about family. Two days were never enough for me to do all the things I wanted to do with my family so I was mindful of each moment, how it was spent and what it meant. Since I spent so much time during the week being their mother, I liked to set that role to the side for a while and focus on also being their friend. In my eyes, it was just as important that they saw me as a trusted friend, a relationship I had with mother and father, that made our relationships that much more special.

Chapter 12

Putting the idea that my husband may or may not settle down one day out of my mind was very liberating. It brought a much-needed end to eight long years of pushing and hoping for something that had always been completely out of my control despite my continued efforts to try and control it. When I let go, I found myself in a place where I could peacefully accept my responsibilities as a mother within the framework of our marriage.

Being primarily responsible for our children was honestly not something that had ever crossed my mind when I got married. I had not even considered it when our children were born. I thought my husband would naturally just share in the responsibilities of raising our children because he was their father. It never occurred to me that it would take years for him to settle down, and in that time, I would travel an unexpected road to motherhood – a single mother's road to motherhood.

It takes courage, strength, and resolve to raise children and, in my opinion, no one knew that better than the single mother. So, I wanted to learn from them. I wanted to know what they knew about being everything to their children, to themselves, and how they made it all work.

So, I set out to gather a wealth of information on how to play the role of a single mother and put it to work for me and our children.

The first and perhaps most important lesson I learned was to assign our children chores. As you can tell from reading thus far, I did more than the lion's share of the work around my house. I just took it upon myself to take care of nearly everything for our children because, somewhere along the line, I got it into my head that was what I was supposed to do even though that was not what my mother did for me.

Single mothers did not have the capacity to do everything for themselves and their children so they had no choice but to assign chores. It was the only guarantee that all the work that needed to get done around the house did. And, when all hands were on deck, there could be plenty of silly time later for all. If they had figured out that they could not do it all, why hadn't I?

When our children entered kindergarten, my husband began telling me to give our children chores. Assign them a job, he would call it. When I thought of assigning a job, I thought of our dogs but, as it turned out, he was actually on to something.

By assigning their children chores at an early age, single mothers raised their children to be self-sufficient, responsible and they prepared them for the future. That validated that I was actually not doing our children any favors by doing everything for them, even though I thought that was the case. I did chores when I was growing up and I turned out just fine.

At first, our children were given simple chores like picking up after themselves, straightening up their rooms, putting their dirty clothes into the laundry room and turning out the lights when they left a room. None of these were big asks on their part but they translated into huge wins for me. The house stayed organized, their clothes were in the dirty laundry hampers (not on the floor in their rooms) and we saved on the electric bill.

I honestly thought, our children might get angry at me for putting them to work so it was amazing to hear them say they enjoyed doing chores. And, it was even more amazing when they started volunteering for other chores around the house like setting the dinner table or clearing the dishes. Our son and daughter even went so far as to clean the windows in the kitchen.

To continue making it easier for them to help around the house, I arranged the coat closet just off the kitchen. There they could drop their backpacks, coats and shoes when they got home from school instead of dropping them in a pile in the middle of my dining room. I also placed items for them to return to their rooms on the staircase so they could pick them up on their way upstairs.

In exchange for all of their hard work each week, our children received one dollar in allowance.

Their help around the house proved so invaluable that it made me look for other ways in which I could enlist help in other areas of my life. I had so much on my plate each day that it made sense to ensure I was working smarter not harder in every aspect of my life. When I really started looking around at some of the options that were available to me, I could not believe I had not taken advantage of them sooner.

For instance, I discovered that paying someone to grocery shop for me was worth every penny and more of the money I spent. It was a priceless gesture for this woman who was responsible for feeding her family but neither enjoyed grocery shopping nor had the time. I could leisurely grocery-shop from the comfort of my home and then just drive to the store to pick up our groceries for the week. Not only did it save me time but it also saved money for I no longer fell victim to the inevitable impulse buying that resulted from dragging two little children through the grocery store.

Creating a weekly menu, something my mother had done for years, was also a time saver. I never got around to doing that myself because my husband always changed his mind about what he wanted to eat for dinner by the time evening rolled around. But then, I learned that single mothers did this all the time, especially on nights when they had social engagements or after school activities. It took the guess work out of feeding their family's when they were on the run. I went so far as invite our children to choose what they wanted for dinner two nights a week. To no surprise, they chose pizza and turkey tacos, two house favorites.

I also learned that single mothers set up rituals to promote a sense of stability and normalcy within their home that was anything but. This was especially important in the world these days where the very definition of normal changes constantly.

The first ritual, I put into practice, was to include a movie night each week, which I thought was a great idea.

Our children loved the family time together and I loved that I could finally see all the movies that I never had time to watch.

Of all the lessons I learned, the single most important was to keep life simple. I was the first person to admit that I had an uncanny ability to confuse a situation and make it much more complicated than it needed to be. Perhaps, that was because I was once prone to a messy mind. But since I began the practice of mindfulness, I could clearly see that most situations had a simple and a difficult option so I decided to always seek out and put into place the first.

There were so many things with our children's schooling alone that I could have been involved in. Had I done them all I would have been too stressed out to really enjoy each of them as I would have liked. My time was in high demand so I needed to really stop and think about what I volunteered for and when. I resolved then and there to let the stay-at-home mothers do the lion's share of the work. They knew I was a working mother and understood that my time was more limited than theirs. Fortunately, our children did, too.

It was such an interesting exercise to dive into the world of the single mother. For all intents and purposes, my mother was a single mother for the majority of my life. And, I had only briefly known one or two since then but they made the same lasting impression on me that she had. Those women were so strong that I already had great respect for them but I came to have even more after coming to understand what they did and how they did it.

At the end of the day, working mothers need to use many of them same tools when raising their children as single mothers for they need help just as much. In today's society, working mothers are just as busy as single mothers.

After I put these lessons in play with our children, they and my husband showed me an immense amount of respect. Far more respect than when I ran myself around like a crazy woman doing everything for nearly everyone. Putting my foot down earned me the respect I had longed for the last five years.

Chapter 13

There is an old saying: "If you love something, set it free, if it returns, it was meant to be, if it continues to fly, let it soar, and have faith that God has something better in store."

For a dozen or so years, I longed for the fairy tale marriage and family with the man I saw as my Prince Charming. I believed that in his heart, he wanted the same thing with me and our children but something was always holding him back. And so, I let the dream go.

As fate would have it, not long after that day the most peculiar thing happened. My husband realized that his wife and family brought more to his life than any amount of socializing ever could.

It all started when my husband abruptly stopped conjuring up any excuse every afternoon for why he had to drive to town. Nothing in his daily routine had changed yet, out of the blue, if he needed to run to the bank or stop by the post office, he did so at his lunch break. Or, if he had errands to run, he grouped them together and only left the house (with the entire family) a few days a week or ran them on Saturday. He even started saying he enjoyed being home as much as our children did.

To my pleasant surprise, he began waking up early and letting me sleep in. He programmed the coffee maker so a steaming hot pot of coffee was ready and waiting for me when I got out of bed. My husband prepared our daughter's pancakes and poured our son's bowl of cereal which he sat with him. He went on to start driving with us to school in the mornings and occasionally picking our children up in the afternoons. My husband also went so far as to set a recurring alarm on his cell phone that went off ten minutes before it was time to pick them up.

Even though my husband was still cooped up in the house all week, it was no longer entirely his doing that moved us out of the house on the weekends. He also sometimes recommended that when we did need to go out and run errands, we went home before our children could ask or he recommended our errands waited until another day. He concurred with our children that it was always nice to stay home on the weekends.

My husband said he felt a shift in our world, as he described it, and I could not have agreed more. He was slowly becoming more involved in our children's lives because of which our children were finally getting to know their father despite having lived with him for five years already.

As a result of changing his behavior, my husband's bonds with our son and daughter are growing stronger each day as he now seems to realize what he was missing out on all these years. Slow and steady is his pace, which is we accept, given that is how we will all win this race.

The relationship between my husband and I is also growing stronger. We are becoming friends again and, with that, rekindling our romance. He is more engaged in his role of husband than ever before.

There is no doubt, you are asking yourself what changed in our lives that led my husband's clarity and his sudden thirst for family. I wish I could say it was my transformation back into the woman I was before we married and had children, but that would not be the entire truth. Nor would it be if I said it was the freedom he was received when the fairy tale faded away. Perhaps, it was solely the revival of his spirituality.

While I believe they all had some impact in one way or another, the honest truth is that it was really his actions alone that made all the difference. He had to want to change, when he was ready to change, and as our luck would have it, he finally decided it was time for him to change as I was writing the final chapter of this book.

Now instead of hoping and praying that my husband will change, I hope and pray that he will keep up his changes. Something tells me that even though he tried before, in the past and failed, he will not fail this time. He is committed to making himself a better husband, father, son, friend, brother, and person. I still do not tell him as often as I should how very proud of him I am and thank you. I think I will start today.

In eight months, I will turn fifty years old.

As I have always done when a birthday approaches, I am sitting back and reevaluating my life. I have cleaned my plate of much-unneeded, dead weight by settling down my messy mind, putting my house in order and finding a state of mindfulness. And I have had already cleaned and polished my presentation with a new hairdo, a little makeup, and some new clothes. Out with the old and in with the new. As I go into this next birth year, I am consciously setting my new plate in such a way as to make this my greatest year ever.

My husband spent five years sitting on the sidelines of our marriage and family but now he is in the game. So, in the middle of my plate, I will place my two children, myself, and my husband – the centers of my world. We will be surrounded by my family and dear friends.

Along the edges of my plate, I will place tokens to remind me of the woman I have become.
First, a symbol of mindfulness to remind me of the messy mind I once had and next to it is a microphone to remind me to speak clearly, confidently, and fearlessly. There is a white flag to remind me to ask for help and a card upon which the word thanks is written to remind me to always live a life of gratitude. Lastly, I candle that burns in the hopes that one day all my dreams will come true.

Any remaining items that once occupied my plate such as cowardliness, silence, servitude, and compliance no longer have a place. They never served me well so I have let them go.

As I look to my future, it is much more hopeful than just one month ago. And, if my husband and I can both hold true to our recent changes, then the sky is our limit.

When I was a little girl dreaming of the day I would be a wife and a mother, the path I assumed I would travel looked tremendously different from the road I took. I had high hopes and expectations that were born from the stories I had read and the movies I had watched. They led me to believe that my life just might be something out of a fairy tale. But I lost sight of that and convinced myself that the fairy tale really was not possible after all. Fortunately, I am a little bit older and hopefully a whole lot wiser now so I can see that just because my life did not go as planned does not mean I am not getting to live my fairy tale.

My road to motherhood was completely unexpected but I know in my heart that I am better because of it. I am more appreciative of being a mother for its freedom, its surprises, and for its sheer unpredictability then I imagine I would have been otherwise. And, now that I have a husband who is settling down and the family I always dreamed about is clearly within site, I would not change a single step of my unexpected road to motherhood for anything in this world.

CPSIA information can be obtained
at www.ICGtesting.com
Printed in the USA
LVHW010157110720
660356LV00019B/810

9 781645 362234